Broken Hearts:
Like Mother, Like Daughter

*A Spiritual Call for
Equality in Health Care*

THE HONORABLE
Alma G. Stallworth, PhD

Copyrighted Material
Broken Hearts: Like Mother, Like Daughter
A Spiritual Call to Action for Equality in Health Care
Copyright © 2015, 2018 Alma G. Stallworth, PhD. All Rights Reserved.

No part of this publication may be reproduced, stored in a retrieval system or transmitted, in any form or by any means – electronic, mechanical, photocopying, recording, or otherwise – without prior written permission from the publisher, except for the inclusion of brief quotations in a review.

For information about this title or to order other books and/or electronic media, contact the publisher:

Atkins & Greenspan Writing
18530 Mack Avenue, Suite 166
Grosse Pointe Farms, MI 48236
www.atkinsgreenspan.com

ISBN 978-1-945875-50-2 (Hardcover)
ISBN 978-1-945875-51-9 (Paperback)
ISBN 978-1-945875-52-6 (eBook)

Printed in the United States of America

Cover and Interior design: Van-garde Imagery, Inc.

*"Wait on the Lord: be of good courage and he
Shall strengthen thine heart: wait, I say, on the Lord."*

Psalm 27:14

Dedicated to my Sisters:
Carolyn Cunningham
Ila Blake
Merle Coleman
Debra Singley

Introduction

THIS BOOK IS A call to action for you to help advocate for equality in health care for all Americans. It is written from my heart and soul, and inspired by the personal anguish of losing my mother to the same disease that has caused me tremendous physical suffering as well.

Through our suffering, I witnessed the vast discrepancies in the quality of health care that Americans receive. Those discrepancies are rooted in socioeconomic status. The care and coverage that I received for multiple, ongoing medical problems has been far more comprehensive than what my mother was given. The reasons are many. The reality is singular: every person should receive equally excellent health care, regardless of their financial or educational or political stature.

The cost of inequality in American health care is sickness, suffering, and deaths that could have been prevented. I hope to inform you and inspire you to take action to help reform this oft-debated issue.

At the same time, this book is a testament to God's miraculous ways. It is a testament that prayer works. On these pages, I testify to the power of miracles to heal, as I overcame significant odds of having my severely handicapped bowel function restored to normalcy. I am living, breathing proof that faith is the foundation for healing. That's why the first edition of this book was called, *Waiting on the Lord*.

My family has waited on the Lord to heal us and bless us with His mercy.

"But faith without works is dead," the Bible tells us in James 2:14-26 in the New King James Version. "What does it profit, my brethren, if someone says he has faith but does not have works? Can faith save him? If a brother or sister is naked and destitute of daily food, and one of you says to them, 'Depart in peace, be warmed and filled,' but you do not give them the things which are needed for the body, what does it profit? Thus also faith by itself, if it does not have works, is dead."

The formula for getting results is to combine faith with action.

And as a witness to my mother's suffering and inadequate health care – compared to the high quality care that I received – the dramatic inequities in our health care system require our urgent attention and action. That's why, after sharing our family story in this book, I am providing action steps that you can take to advocate for better health and improved health care for everyone.

This book is entitled *Broken Hearts: Like Mother, Like Daughter, A Spiritual Call to Action For Equality in Health Care* for several reasons.

When I say "broken hearts," the meaning is literal and figurative. My mother and I literally suffered with broken hearts due to congestive heart failure, and I have endured a broken heart in a figurative sense by watching her suffer and lose her life to this disease.

This experience has shown me that life-saving treatments are available. Many caring nurses, physicians, surgeons, and other health care professionals have provided excellent treatments that improved my physical well-being, and actually saved my life.

At the same time, I know that God continues to orchestrate every step along my journey. Prayer truly works wonders. Keep the faith in God's power to make miracles happen for you, your family, and our

Introduction

world. Keep close to your heart the comforting words of Hebrews 11:1 in the King James Version of the Bible:

"Now faith is the substance of things hoped for, the evidence of things not seen." I have learned that through faith, you will see the evidence of God's grace in the form of healing.

My wish is for you to read our story, learn about congestive heart failure, and feel inspired to take exquisite care of yourself and your family, as well as advocate that the best health care be provided for all Americans, regardless of their socioeconomic status.

Thank you for taking time to answer my spiritual call to action for equality in health care.

Alma G. Stallworth, PhD

Contents

Introduction vii

Chapter 1   Broken Hearts: Like Mother, Like Daughter 1

Chapter 2   Lisbon Singley: My Mother's Story 7

Chapter 3   Alma Stallworth, PhD: My Story 11

Chapter 4   Public Policies That Impact Golden Years 19

Inspiration 23

Sources: 25

Biography 27

Chapter 1

Broken Hearts: Like Mother, Like Daughter

BOTH MY MOTHER AND I have suffered from congestive heart failure. Before I dive deeper into our personal stories, I want to answer a question that I'm often asked:

What is Congestive Heart Failure?

As you probably know, the heart is a pump that keeps blood pulsing through the body to nourish our cells and keep us alive. It pushes blood through our veins and arteries to deliver oxygen and nutrients to our brains, our lungs, our limbs, and every cell in our bodies. Without a heartbeat, the blood cannot pump through the body to provide everything that our organs, bones, tissues, and muscles need to function. You can compare the human heart to the engine in a car. Without an engine, a car will not run. When the engine fails, the car stalls.

Congestive heart failure is a condition that weakens the heart, reducing its ability to efficiently keep blood pumping – and flowing back to the heart in a continuous cycle of circulation through the body. As a result, adequate oxygen and nutrients fail to reach the cells, and the heart becomes overworked. Fluid can accumulate throughout the body, causing swelling in the feet, ankles, and legs. Fluid can also pool in the lungs, causing "pulmonary congestion." Meanwhile, the cells suffer because they are not receiving enough oxygen and nutrients. All of these problems can result in hospitalizations, complications, and ultimately, death.

Unfortunately, heart disease is the number one cause of death in America, according to the US Centers for Disease Control and Prevention. To provide some perspective, the CDC says that in 2016, the most recent year for which statistics are available, 635,260 Americans died of heart disease. The second leading cause of death was cancer, taking 598,038 lives. Notice the significant decrease in the number of the third leading cause of death: accidents, which claimed 161,374 lives, the CDC reports.

The United States is not alone. Heart disease is also the top cause of death around the world. In fact, the World Health Organization reports that ischaemic heart disease (reduced blood supply to the heart) resulting from arteries blocked by fat and cholesterol, caused 8.7 million deaths, or 15.5 percent of total deaths.

Clearly, heart disease is a major health threat everywhere.

If you have congestive heart failure, you're not alone. Nearly six million Americans are living with it today, according to WebMD. Every year, about 670,000 people are diagnosed with heart failure, WebMD says, and it's the leading cause of hospitalization for men and women age 65 and older.

Younger people can also be at risk, and some common illnesses, including high blood pressure, diabetes, thyroid disease, and kidney disease, can all cause congestive heart failure. The condition can also affect people who are diagnosed with heart defects at birth. Some medications used to treat other conditions, including cancer, can cause congestive heart failure. Similarly, obesity, an abnormal heartbeat, sleep apnea, some viruses, excessive alcohol consumption, and cigarette smoking can also increase the risk for heart failure, according to the Mayo Clinic.

You can prevent your chances of developing heart disease by living a healthy lifestyle that includes: eating healthy foods that are low in sodium, saturated fat, and cholesterol; exercising and being active for 30 minutes or more every day; keeping your weight at a healthy level for your height and age; avoiding smoking cigarettes and inhaling second-hand smoke; maintaining your blood pressure in the normal range; keeping other health conditions under control; getting regular checkups with your physician and making sure you visit the doctor right away if any new problems develop; and reducing or avoiding stress.

Symptoms, Diagnosis & Treatment

Sometimes people with congestive heart failure endure it for a long time, so their condition is called chronic. For others, it strikes suddenly. According to the Mayo Clinic, symptoms can include: shortness of breath; a rapid or irregular heartbeat; fatigue and weakness that result in diminished ability to exercise and even fainting; swelling in the abdomen, legs, ankles, and feet; weight gain due to this swelling; a greater need to urinate at night; coughing or wheezing that produces blood-streaked phlegm or foamy, pink mucus; problems with concentration and alertness; nausea and/or loss of appetite; and chest pain in the case of a heart attack.

Your doctor can diagnose congestive heart failure with a variety of tests that include: a blood test; a chest Xray; an electrocardiogram or ECG that measures your heart's electrical activity by using sound waves to assess your heart's function; a stress test conducted as you walk on a treadmill while attached to an ECG machine that measures your heart's activity; a CT scan that Xrays your body and records images of your heart and chest; an MRI that uses a magnetic field and radio waves to capture detailed images of your heart; a coronary angiogram that involves inserting a tube through a blood vessel in the groin so doctors can explore your heart; and a myocardial biopsy that removes heart tissue for analysis.

Diagnosis of heart failure does not mean immediate death. It simply means that the heart is not functioning as efficiently as it should. And without treatment, the problem will get worse.

Treatment for heart failure involves two steps. The first step requires treating and controlling the problem – such as high blood pressure – that may be triggering the heart failure. The second step is taking medication – usually a combination of medications – that can help the heart function as efficiently as possible. The medications also help reduce the chances of sudden death.

You may be wondering, "What is the difference between heart failure and heart attack?" They are both heart disease, and can result from the same culprits. However, a heart attack happens suddenly after an artery that feeds blood to the heart becomes blocked, which damages the heart tissue, and makes the heart unable to function properly. On the other hand, heart failure tends to develop over time.

This is a chronic condition that gradually gets worse. Fortunately, medications can enhance wellness and prolong life for people who have congestive heart failure.

Like Mother, Like Daughter

My family's experience with congestive heart failure has provided a case study in the vast and unfortunate differences between the type of health care that people receive based on their socioeconomic status.

My mother had Medicare, which is the health insurance coverage that the government provides for people who are age 65 and older. In contrast, as a retired state lawmaker, I was covered by both Medicare and Blue Cross Blue Shield. My mother and I received different coverage for hospitalization, surgery, and therapeutic prescription drugs.

After several heart attacks, Mom received home care supplemented by the Department of Social Services, which provided a visiting nurse, a part-time housekeeper, and physical therapy. She also received Meals on Wheels, a food nutritional program provided by the Wayne County Office on Aging. In contrast, I received private nursing provided through my insurance. Other basic assistance for my home care was given by family members, primarily my husband.

Cultural beliefs and practices among our senior citizens can also influence behaviors that result in not receiving the maximum coverage and benefits. For example, like many seniors, Mom refused to apply to the Michigan Department of Social Services to receive approval for a medication card that required only one dollar for each prescription filled. Instead, she was purchasing half of each prescription with an independent pharmacy using a credit card. After learning of her prescription needs, I submitted an application to Social Services on her behalf, providing the required information, which was basically verification of income. This significantly reduced her health care expenses, as she was no longer paying the higher prices for prescription medications, and instead paid only one dollar.

However, had I not advocated for her, she would have continued to shoulder this tremendous financial burden of paying for expensive medications and taking double the time to go to the pharmacy. I share this particular aspect of our story to implore you to assist seniors in understanding what coverage and benefits are available that until now they may have overlooked or avoided.

On the following pages, I will describe the need for family support, prayer, faith, and endurance that extended our lives with the courage and hope to overcome. This book also provides an opportunity to thank the many friends and family members who rendered their prayers and positive thoughts throughout our illness and recovery.

Please join me as I share with you a closer look at my life, my mother's life, and the many differences in the types and quality of care we each received, as well as our differences in cure and recovery.

Chapter 2

Lisbon Singley: My Mother's Story

LISBON SINGLEY MOVED TO Detroit with her husband Enoch Coleman, a US military veteran, and her family in 1939. At that time, she had three daughters: Ila, Carole Coleman, and me, Alma (Russell) Coleman. Throughout her life, my mother had three husbands: Charles Russell, Enoch Coleman, and Adolf Singley. Even though we were half-sisters, we were raised as one family.

My dad, Charles Russell, met my mother in Little Rock, Arkansas, where she was pursuing her high school diploma – because her little town of Biscuit, Arkansas had no high school. My dad's family owned a construction business that provided home repairs, painting, and wallpapering. Because he was working, he was able to assist with schooling and other personal needs, which allowed her to attend school full time. After a short courtship, they were married, producing their first and only child together, me, Alma Russell. The marriage had its ups and downs due to their youthful immaturity. After their separation and divorce, Mother moved to Des Moines, Iowa, where she met Enoch Coleman; they married and had three children.

Later, upon moving to Detroit, they found employment, but housing was quite a problem. For families with children, options were limited. Rental properties were difficult to find. At one point, Mother was tricked out of $50, after making a deposit on a non-existent rental property. As a result, we stayed for a number of months with my mother's friend, who was also a former resident of Little Rock, Arkansas. My stepfather, Enoch Coleman, was eventually hired by Federal Motor Company.

For many years, my mother worked as a beautician, operating her own beauty shop. She also served as a teacher at one of the local beauty schools. Due to her long hours of work, I often had to substitute her attendance at school functions, and supervise my sisters at home, ensuring that they completed their homework and household chores.

After Enoch Coleman preceded her in death, she married Adolf Singley and birthed another daughter, Debra Singley.

Years later, while Mother was employed as a clerical worker at the Herman Kiefer Health Center, her heart illness started. Debra lived with her during her critical illness. Family members often felt that her illness was partly due to the stress and strain of three unsuccessful marriages. This included two divorces without sufficient child support by either husband, as well as her struggle with securing adequate employment. In spite of these difficulties, she continued to have faith in God, praying for strength and endurance.

With the added support of Wayne County Human Services, Mother had sufficient help. During this time, it was difficult for me to contribute because I was living in Hampton, Virginia, due to my husband's employment at the Veterans Hospital. Upon returning home to Detroit, I became more aware of mother's needs due to her illness. Additional commitments by family members were needed.

As many adult children experience, it was very difficult to commit to continued involvement because of other personal demands on time and resources. All of my sisters were employed or in school. Three of us were married with our own children. Oftentimes we were inconsistent with care for our mother, because our other family responsibilities were so great.

However, amid the uncertainty of family members being available for a consistent care schedule, additional support was provided by friends who were members at Bethel AME Church, where we attended as a family and were members for many years. Because of my mother's belief in God, as well as her faith and trust in Him, she instilled in us the power of prayer and deep faith. She remained active in participating in church activities as well as attending services.

Mother also enjoyed the assistance of friends who provided transportation as needed. As a dedicated member of the choir, she attended many of the practice meetings. She shared the blessings of God's love by teaching Sunday school class each week. Even though her illness limited her abilities, she was also dedicated to attending Sunday services, making it a high priority from week to week. Visitors were few because most of her friends were seniors with similar problems. This made church visits as well as health assistance vitally important.

The neighborhood where we lived began to change and an increasing need developed for a strong community organization. Her illness did not stop her from becoming actively involved in the efforts to organize. She also served as secretary for the Virginia Park Neighborhood Association. Friends and neighbors volunteered to provide transportation to the various meetings.

Mother also dedicated her time to caring for her pets and flowers. She enjoyed cooking, even though she was dependent on a wheelchair to get around. Her home had two levels, and her heart problem made it very difficult to climb the stairs. As a result, the upstairs bedroom furniture was moved to the dining room on the first floor to eliminate the need for stair-climbing. An additional challenge was having access to the bathroom. She loved tub baths and would often sneak upstairs to take a bath when alone.

Unfortunately, Medicare did not cover eyeglasses or dental services. This meant a family member had to provide the necessary financing to meet those needs. Being the oldest sister, I usually responded.

At the end of the summer, scheduling care for our mother was challenging because Ila and I had to return to our work schedules. Ila was a teacher at Cass Technical High School in Detroit, and I was resuming my legislative schedule. We worked very hard to develop other arrangements. Finally, I was able to secure patient care at the Boulevard Nursing Home, which was quite close to our homes. When one of the clerks called to announce approval for admittance, Mother became very upset, refusing the services. She immediately went into the kitchen to cook one of her favorite meals. I think her reactions were typical of seniors who wanted to stay in their own homes, where they feel secure and safe.

She was, however, moved into the nursing home. While there, Mom was able to get the revolving care and assistance she needed. As a family, we are inspired by Mom's faithfulness, love, and trust in the Lord, which provided her endurance and bolstered her belief in God's mercy. She passed at 84 years of age in 1997.

Chapter 3

Alma Stallworth, PhD: My Story

LIKE MY MOTHER, I married at 19 years of age. However, unlike her, I have sustained our marriage for over 60-plus years. My determination was based on my commitment to raise my two sons with a firm base of family support by ensuring that two caring parents were in the home and most importantly in their lives. This endeavor was successful because both my husband and I shared that commitment and worked to make it happen.

During my middle years, I enjoyed good health, even though I was overweight.

In 1986, I was diagnosed as a Type 2 Diabetic, which required me to take a pill and test my blood sugar every day. Diet was also important. When I experienced swelling of my legs and ankles, my podiatrist's Xrays revealed that I had a serious problem and needed to see a primary doctor. I scheduled an appointment in June of 2011 at Henry Ford Hospital with a primary doctor. After a physical and testing, it was recommended that I schedule a colon scan.

The colon scan identified cancer cells in my colon, which required immediate surgery. I was scheduled in mid-July of 2011. The first surgery identified an added condition that confirmed a blockage that required additional surgery. I was advised that after the second surgery, an ostomy would be required. I learned the ostomy required a surgery to have a bag inserted in my stomach to accommodate bowel movements; I became scared and nervous because I was not familiar with such a condition. Enduring this change was a nightmare. I was told this impairment had no definite end.

The second surgery was performed in September by Dr. Melissa Times, a member of the Colon Rectal Surgeons at Henry Ford Hospital. During my hospital stay, I suffered a heart attack. Doctors inserted a stent, which is a tube made of mesh wire that opens up a coronary artery that had been clogged and was therefore blocking blood flow to the heart. During the stent procedure, doctors confirmed that I had a heart problem.

Many times when I was in critical condition, I felt I was at death's door. Due to the surgeries, I lost 20 pounds, which lowered my blood sugar. Only prayer and faith sustained me as I suffered pain and uncertainty. Reverend Dorinda Phillips, a minister of Oak Grove AME Church, provided spiritual support by visiting me in the hospital. She spent time at my bedside, reading scriptures, and praying for my recovery. Other church members and friends sent messages of good will through cards and phone calls.

Complicating my situation was that doctors also removed a hernia while I was hospitalized. The close proximity of the incisions made my recuperation at home even more difficult.

For three months, a skilled basic nurse practitioner provided health care services during my recovery from colon surgery. Unfortunately, I suffered continuing problems with the maintenance and care of the ostomy. During those 90 days, the nurse provided the interventions that I needed by recommending an ostomy specialist who could advise me regarding the care of the attachment, as well as other options for supplies.

Another important element was the prescription drugs ordered by several doctors: my surgeon, my cardiologist, and my primary doctor. Daily medications were a challenge because they often had side effects.

Additional care was provided by my dear husband, who worked with the nurse to understand procedures for caring for my incisions. Over time, I learned how to empty and maintain the ostomy. However, the challenges of continuing leakage and splitting of the bag were very stressful. This condition continued for five months. I pursued help from the Specialists of St. John Providence Hospital and the Henry Ford Health System Wound Care Centers. Neither offered a remedy, but provided additional information regarding supplies.

Dr. Times determined that the ostomy should be removed after learning of my continued need for a successful resolution for my problems. The surgery was performed in February of 2012. I later learned such reversal or removal of the bag was very uncommon. Most patients have to endure this impairment for life. However, the successful removal illustrates the advancement in medical procedures. I experienced very few health problems after the surgery.

My message is one of health and healing, which were provided through the spirit of God within me. He has continued to bless my body and soul with the power of healing. With these words of life, I render thanks to the Lord for blessed results, because I know I have been embraced in God's presence, making me feel safe and secure.

For the following three months, I enrolled in the William Clay Ford Center for Athletic Medicine to engage in rehab sessions that provided exercise three times a week. Medicare paid for these sessions because of my age. As a result, progress was made in strengthening my heart and my legs, while also lowering my blood pressure.

Based on my progress, I was able to travel to Dayton, Ohio, to attend the Regional Conference of Top Ladies of Distinction. My dear friend, Delores May, consented to drive and share accommodations during the conference. We had an excellent time attending the various meetings, and visiting discount stores.

During our drive back to Detroit, I experienced extreme shortness of breath. Delores called 911 for assistance. I was immediately admitted to the Intensive Care Unit of Dayton Health Center. My son, Dr. K.B. Stallworth, and his wife Nicole drove from Detroit. Many of the women attending the conference immediately came to my side, providing prayer and support. I remained in intensive care for five days. Even though I wasn't a resident of Dayton, I received excellent care. An additional stent was placed in my heart due to the recurring blockage. My husband drove from Detroit and remained at my side the entire time, along with our son, Representative Thomas Stallworth III, who was a member of the Michigan House of Representatives.

Heart and lung ailments, and other associated health correction procedures, resulted in substantial loss of weight and strength. During Thanksgiving of 2012, I suffered another heart attack and was rushed to the emergency room at Providence Hospital. After I was stabilized, the attending cardiologist shared the terrible news – based on their findings – that immediate open heart surgery must be scheduled. This recommendation was very frightening to me as well my family. The assisting doctor described the procedure in detail to ensure we had a clear understanding. He indicated that an incision would be cut from the top of the adnominal section, cracking my rib open to remove my heart, placing me on life support while my heart is removed, repaired, and reinserted into my chest. This surgery was projected to be a six-hour procedure.

Both my sons, Thomas and Keith, feared that I could not endure the stress of such a procedure after the extensive colon surgery and additional heart attacks I had suffered the previous year. They also feared that the intense rehabilitation that I would require would be very difficult. Both advised me not to sign any agreements until they explored other options.

My son, Thomas Stallworth, intervened. I was transferred to Harper University Hospital in the Detroit Medical Center, and referred to Theodore L. Schreiber MD, Chief of the Division of Cardiology and the President of the DMC Cardiovascular Institute. Dr. Schreiber provided a less invasive procedure. Two additional stents were placed in my heart. Within one week, I was discharged and returned home. For the next three weeks, a visiting nurse provided services, testing my blood pressure and weight and monitoring my medications.

I share this experience to stress the critical need for interventions, as well as supportive help by family members when medical decisions are pending. This intervention is especially important for elderly patients. Doctors are not always sensitive to previous ailments or additional required treatments.

I believe healing is more than the physical condition. It is the renewal of beliefs in self, along with a positive attitude that affirms a will to live. Such understanding has blessed me spiritually and physically. Through God's mercy, I have survived.

Returning home, I again enjoyed successful recovery. In September, we planned a road trip, accompanied by my husband's brother and sister-in-law to our timeshare vacation home in Atlantic

Beach, North Carolina. It was an excellent trip. While driving there, we stopped overnight to break up the time for rest and meals. The resort was right on the Atlantic Ocean, which offered access to the beach, and offered swimming and sunbathing. For the first time, we visited the Golden Corral Buffet and Grill, a very enjoyable restaurant.

The success of my road trip inspired my doctors and my husband to approve that I take an additional trip to Orlando, Florida in early December of 2013. We once again enjoyed our time share for a week. During our visit, I was able to Christmas shop, tour the city, and enjoy the surrounding areas, which included a pool with leisure accommodations. We traveled by plane, which took only a couple of hours each way.

In preparation for Christmas, I decorated a full Christmas tree, wrapped gifts, and made treats for my grandchildren, whom I expected to visit on Christmas Eve. Unfortunately, I had another heart attack on Christmas Eve and was rushed to Harper University Hospital DMC Emergency. After a transfer to Intensive Care, I stayed for 10 days, from Christmas Eve until New Year's Day. Two more stents were placed in my heart to open another blockage. Once again, a visiting nurse was assigned to monitor my recuperation at home.

After discharge, I felt well for six months and was able to enjoy traditional activities. I was even able to volunteer and serve as Chair of the Women for Duggan Committee that supported Mike Duggan as a candidate for Mayor of Detroit. However, in early September of 2013, I suffered another flare-up, which required hospitalization and an additional procedure that involved placing a balloon in the same valve in my heart.

This was a similar procedure that opened the recurring blockage. I continue to require cardiovascular visits with extensive medications that include aspirin, blood thinners, and high blood pressure pills, as well as other medications. A recommended controlled diet was immediately implemented.

"I trust in the steadfast love of God," says Psalms 52:8. The greatest influence in enduring the continuing health challenges is releasing all problems and concerns to God's will.

I understand many lawmakers in Congress and the State Legislature are dedicated to improving the health care services for children and families. However, in spite of these efforts, unmet health challenges still need attention. Even with the best insurance – Blue Cross Blue Shield – I still felt helpless because I needed others to help save my life. The Lord has continued to bless and keep me. I had no additional flare-ups during 2014, and my health continues to demonstrate that the Lord is in charge.

Chapter 4

Public Policies That Impact Golden Years

Public Policies That Impact Golden Years
A Report published by
REPRESENTATIVE ALMA STALLWORTH
1974

The Golden Years!

Improved living conditions and advanced medical care extended the life experience of us all and made senior citizens an increasing percentage of the population nationally as well as within the State of Michigan. Many realize that a longer life is a mixed blessing. For many it represents a delay in the onset of a multitude of difficult problems. At one time or another, all aging persons face failing health. Even those who manage a marginal income due to savings and investments have been denied health care until they can claim impoverishment.

More than 25 percent of those over 65 years of age must prove they live on sub-poverty incomes. Those living on a fixed income or a low income are being crushed by inflation that has significantly increased food prices in Detroit. Many of those who have worked all of their lives and have contributed to pension funds are disappointed to learn that their benefits are either non-existent or only a percentage of what they anticipated.

Government's Responsibility to the Elderly

I have always been one of the growing numbers of elected officials who believe the aged have a right to quality health care and a decent standard of living.

It is the government's responsibility to ensure that right. I have continued to work with other clients at the local, state, and federal levels to create change in the system. Each level of government has its own appropriate role in meeting the needs of senior citizens. The federal government, for example, because of its vast tax revenues, is the most capable of providing direct financial assistance to the Social Security program, as well as the Supplemental Security Income (SSI) program, which provides benefits for disabled adults and children whose income and resources are limited. People 65 and older who are within certain financial limits but do not have disabilities can also qualify for SSI benefits.

I'm sharing this 1974 report today because very few changes have been made to revise the Public Policies. This is a call for action! Many of the same challenges that I cited over four decades ago continue to leave Americans with unmet needs.

The best solution today is for younger people to rally the cause. Many do not relate to the problem as outlined, until it becomes a family problem that affects a mother, father, and other family relatives. As the years go by, health care prevention and maintenance become a personal problem. Let's address it now!

Let your voice be heard by writing to your local, state, and federal lawmakers. The people who represent you in your state legislature, as well as the United States House of Representatives and the United States Senate in Washington, DC were elected as your leaders in our government. Call and email your elected officials to demand action on equal health care for everyone, including seniors.

Remember, knowledge is power! So learn and live!

Inspiration

"God is the strength of my heart and my portion forever."

– Psalm 73:26

The Lord's Prayer
　　Our Father which art in heaven,
　　Hallowed be thy name,
　　Thy Kingdom come
　　Thy will be done in earth, as it is in heaven.
　　Give us this day our daily bread
　　And forgive us our debts, as we forgive our debtors.
　　And lead us not into temptation, but deliver us from evil:
　　For thine is the kingdom, and the power,
　　and glory, forever.
　　Amen
　　Matthew 6:9-13 (KJV)

Broken Hearts: Like Mother, Like Daughter

"Trust in the Lord, and do good ...
And he will give you the desires of your heart."

Psalms: 37:3-4

"The tongue of the wise brings healing."

Proverbs 12:18

Sources:

https://www.worldatlas.com/articles/top-ten-leading-causes-of-death-in-the-world.html
https://www.mayoclinic.org/
https://www.webmd.com/

Biography

THE HONORABLE ALMA G. Stallworth, PhD is an exemplary leader whose values and policies are rooted in faith, family, and fairness for people everywhere. Born in Little Rock, Arkansas, in 1932, she moved to Detroit, Michigan, as a child. Academic excellence enabled her to graduate from Northeastern High School at age 15, and she attended Wayne State University.

In 1951, she married Thomas F. Stallworth, Jr. and they are now celebrating 67 years of marriage. Their two sons, Thomas F. Stallworth III and Keith B. Stallworth, and their wives have blessed the couple with grandchildren and great-grandchildren as well.

Dr. Stallworth is best known for serving in the Michigan House of Representatives. She was first elected in 1970 and served until 2005, including 18 years as Chair of the powerful Committee of Public Utilities.

She is also celebrated as the founder of the Black Caucus Foundation of Michigan in 1985. The non-profit organization sponsored an Intern Program for college students and founded the Drug Free Youth in Detroit Program. The longtime Bethel AME Church member has also led youth groups in Africa.

After retirement, she became a summa cum laude doctoral graduate with great distinction from Chelsea University in London, England, where she earned a Master's in Health Promotion & Education, and a PhD in Business Administration.

Dr. Stallworth has authored several books, including: her memoir, *Legacy of a Lawmaker: Inspired by Faith & Family*, and *Broken Hearts: Like Mother, Like Daughter, A Spiritual Call for Equality in Health Care*.

www.ingramcontent.com/pod-product-compliance
Lightning Source LLC
Chambersburg PA
CBHW030104100526
44591CB00008B/270